SIMPLIFIED LITURGIES
FOR
CONTEMPLATIVE WORSHIP

SIMPLIFIED LITURGIES
FOR CONTEMPLATIVE WORSHIP

Sandy Smyth

XULON PRESS

Xulon Press
2301 Lucien Way #415
Maitland, FL 32751
407.339.4217
www.xulonpress.com

© 2019 by Sandy Smyth
Afterword and Appendix added June 2020.

All rights reserved solely by the author. The author guarantees all contents are original and do not infringe upon the legal rights of any other person or work. No part of this book may be reproduced in any form without the permission of the author. The views expressed in this book are not necessarily those of the publisher.

Unless otherwise indicated, Scripture quotations taken from the Holy Bible, New International Version (NIV). Copyright © 1973, 1978, 1984, 2011 by Biblica, Inc.™. Used by permission. All rights reserved.

Permissions and Resources, Scripture readings NIV, Book of Common Prayer, album *Jesus Remember Me* by the London Fox Taize Choir, *Chants de Taize* **2018–2019**, *The 2017 Iona Abbey Worship Book*, and the 1966 *Worship in Song: a Friends Hymnal*. **All words not mine are italicized.** Internet references are documented in Cited Works.

Printed in the United States of America.

ISBN-13: 978-1-5456-6873-3

CONTENTS

Foreword... ix

Chapter 1. Feed My Sheep 1
Envisioning a Contemplative Worship Movement.

Chapter 2. Simplify the Order of Service 5
Creating time for Silence by using less, but more powerful words.

Chapter 3. Order of Service Comparisons 9
Taize and other resources for Contemplative Worship.

Chapter 4. The Iona Abbey Worship Book............. 19
Incorporating Iona worship texts.

Chapter 5. Synthesis of Worship Patterns.............. 25
Bringing Liturgies together to create meaningful worship experiences.

Chapter 6. Conclusion................................ 35
Adapting the Order of Service to simplify worship.

Afterword. *Creating an online Order of Service for Contemplative Worship* 49

Cited Works 81

Additional Resources.................................... 85

FOREWORD

This little book is an extension of my 2013, 2018 publication of *Sermons Never Preached on the Spirit-led Life*, particularly Chapter 9, Conclusion: the Gift of More Silence in Christian Worship.

I believe that the Church as an institution must begin to make larger spaces in worship for Silence and Contemplation; otherwise, liturgy is depriving congregants of a closer union with Christ's immediate presence in their souls.

My church is a busy one with many ministries and well-intentioned, active chairpersons. But there is also an emerging group within my church who desire to rest in God in Silence and Contemplation. I belong to that group.

We meet once a week for a time of sharing Scripture, discussion of Fr. Thomas Keating's daily offerings and their meaning to our personal lives, prior to 20 minutes in Silent Contemplation. Taize songs, "Wait for the Lord" and "Bless the Lord, My Soul", accompany the before and after 20 minutes of Silence.

Our souls are greatly nourished by this time of stillness and reflection. As a result of that time in Silence, aware of God's presence, we have become more consciously aligned with Christ's spirit of compassion and loving-kindness.

In 2018, I added a Postface to *Sermons Never Preached* about the Contemplation group within my Episcopal church and how that has become my true worship experience as I attend Sunday church less and less.

My hope is that all parishioners will eventually be provided the opportunity to experience Contemplative Worship, which is why I have written this book.

My objective is to provide clergy, worship planners and lay persons who understand the importance of Contemplative Worship, a resource for simplifying liturgies that include a larger space for Silence and soul-time with Christ.

I do not expect rectors to allow a simplified liturgy for traditional Sunday morning worship, but I do hope they will provide in the weekly schedule a time for a Contemplative Service of 45–50 minutes.

I have found the order of service for Taize worship and Taize songs to be valuable in structuring simplified liturgies. But I also want to include the order of service of my own Episcopal church, yet see it simplified. And, perhaps, incorporate the best of Iona's worship services into it. An eclectic service, yes, but also thoroughly congruent with Christian theology. For more information about the Iona community and style of worship, see "What is Iona?" in Cited Works under Foreword.

What is Taize? The Oxford Dictionary defines Taize worship as:

The style of Christian worship practiced by the ecumenical Taizé community in France, characterized by the repetitive singing of simple harmonized tunes, often in various languages, interspersed with readings, prayers, and periods of silence. Taize is the name of a village in Burgundy, France, where the community was founded in 1949.

I am grateful to my Divinity School colleagues and friends, especially Rev. Steve Blackmer, founder of Church of the Woods, Canterbury, New Hampshire, for their openness to innovate programs that invigorate the worship experience with Contemplation.

Grateful also for my Contemplation group at church who show me what a life transformed by Contemplation looks like.

Sandy Smyth
May 2019

Chapter 1.

FEED MY SHEEP

I envision a Contemplative Worship movement growing within the main church to include worship services online.

The seed has been planted; a thirst and hunger for a return to simple church is sprouting. Courageous clergy are helping people to connect to Christ within themselves, in Nature and in Community in a more authentic, less formal way than that of the main church.

According to an article published by the *Christian Science Monitor* on March 7, 2019, titled, "Alternative Churches: the Future of Religion":

> Church in the woods, laundry church, dinner church: in recent years, churches with non-traditional venues, meeting dates, and demographics have sprung up in the hundreds across the US. As institutionalized religion continues to decline, and people seek meaning and

community in ever-shifting ways, will the alternative church movement become the religion of tomorrow?

The article can also be viewed on YouTube.

These courageous clergy members are feeding the lost sheep of the main church who no longer attend and seek God's presence elsewhere.

What concerns me is, why should anyone feel they have to leave the church to feel spiritually nourished? Why not create alternative worship services within the church that feed the needs of our lost sheep? Why not incorporate another way of worship into the weekly or monthly schedule as some churches do?

Diana Butler Bass who teaches at Virginia Theological Seminary (Episcopal) says of Contemplative Worship:

> *In January 2001, when I was teaching a course at Wesley Seminary in Washington, D.C., a student asked me what I thought the 21st century would be like. Without a moment's hesitation I replied, "Noisy. It will be noisy." So I have been surprised by the silence I have encountered in many churches. As a girl I rarely experienced silence in mainline churches and seldom witnessed acts of prayer. My church had succumbed to writer Richard Rohr's prediction, "When the church is no longer*

teaching the people how to pray, we could almost say it will have lost its reason for existence."

Yet in the congregations I have visited, silence, meditation and contemplation were commonplace, and many new members testified to the spiritual attraction of prayer. Martha, a member of Holy Communion, is one of them. "Not many churches give you real silence, if you think about it. I've come to value it. . . . Encountering God certainly [happens] in silence."

(This article first appeared in *The Christian Century*, September 19, 2006, pp. 25–29. Copyright by the Christian Century Foundation; used by permission. www.christiancentury.org).

I have explored online the presence of Taize forms of worship in a few churches across the country, but hope to see more Contemplative Services like them. I also would like to see those services incorporate the order of service of the denomination they serve, yet simplified, to allow more time for Silence.

In Silence, Contemplation allows space to commune with God and to hear what the Holy Spirit is saying to us and what Christ is asking us to do. Christ is always asking us to put aside our egos to walk in love with others as we would want them to walk with us (Golden Rule).

Contemplation is simply stilling the mind of thoughts and focusing on the word of God, resting in the presence of God, of Christ, of the Holy Spirit deep within the heart. It requires practice to still the mind and let go of thoughts, but well worth the time. The world we live in is frantic, and we have so little soul-time. We need more of it and the church should, in my opinion, provide it.

Because the soul longs for the peace and love of God to fill it, I believe it is the role of the main church to teach the value of Silence and allow it in worship, even if it is present in an alternative service during the week. Liturgy needs to be simplified if we are going to allow a larger space in worship for Silence and Contemplation.

Chapter 2.

SIMPLIFY THE ORDER OF SERVICE

Jesus spent time apart in Silence to commune with his Father. I believe it is critical to spiritual health to do the same, so that we may become co-creators with God in God's evolving universe. The church can provide simplified liturgy in alternate services that includes a larger space for Contemplation.

I am not suggesting an elimination of the order of service. I am suggesting **the use of fewer words!** So much of the liturgy is repetitive from week to week that it loses its meaning and is taken for granted. An example is Holy Communion. Why is it so long when a paragraph would suffice as you will see in the simplified liturgies in this book? Why can't liturgy read like an intelligible poem?

With the use of fewer words, more time can be spent in Silent communion with Christ, listening to his words as we reflect on Scripture. Sermons, too, could have more imagery and fewer words and be reduced to a memorable paragraph or two. Jesus spoke in pithy parables to get his point across and always used imagery and language familiar to his listeners. Why not imitate Jesus' method of parables in our sermons?

Also, why not have shorter hymns? We could sing simple hymns of no more than 2 or 3 lines repeated, which remain in memory with meaning, rather than 6 or 8 lines. Prayers, too, could be shortened. Jesus gave us everything we need in the Lord's Prayer. The Lord's Prayer also provides for the forgiveness of sins, so that absolution in the order of service could be eliminated.

In other words, I am suggesting fewer spoken words in the liturgy, more use of words that have powerful imagery, less pomp, and more natural beauty and simplicity and Silence in worship.

Contrary to the simplified liturgy offered here for consideration, is the traditional liturgy of the mainline churches whose worshipers prefer the current liturgy of their church just the way it is, and some do feel God's presence in it.

Contemplative prayer, on the other hand, helps us to let go of our egocentric thoughts as we experience God's presence and word in our hearts. The more we spend time with Christ, the more we become like Him in our actions.

Contemplation takes practice. Church leaders who practice Contemplation can teach it and slowly introduce parishioners to it in the liturgy.

In the following chapters, I illustrate how adding one or two or three outside resources can enliven the same order of service.

Chapter 3.

ORDER OF SERVICE COMPARISONS

The traditional order of Sunday morning service for most Episcopal churches consists of a greeting, a sentence of Scripture offering thanks and praise, a hymn, an opening prayer, collect, introduction of the Word, Old Testament reading or Psalm, New Testament gospel reading, hymn, sermon, saying of the creed, intercessory prayer, confession of sin, sharing the peace, offertory, the Great Thanksgiving, Lord's Prayer, Eucharist distribution of bread and wine, prayer, hymn, blessing, dismissal. All parts flow together to enhance the theme of the service.

My suggestion for an alternate Contemplative Worship Service is a simplified liturgy of the above that incorporates the Taize format and songs that also fit the theme of the seasons, Holy days, or events.

Calvin College has designed a Lenten Taize Service in the following format (see Calvin College in Cited Works, Chapter 3):

Welcome

Gathering Song, Jesus Remember Me

Silent Prayer

Meditation upon Scripture

Sung Refrain, Bless the Lord, My Soul (Psalm 103)— all on refrain, cantor on verses

Romans 10

Prayers

Sung Refrain, O Lord, Hear My Prayer (sing verse 1 only)

Prayers of Intercession (in 3 sections, interspersed with the sung refrain)

Sung Refrain, O Lord, Hear My Prayer (sing verse 1 only)

The Lord's Prayer. Sung Refrain, O Lord, Hear My Prayer (sing verses 1 and 2)

Sending

Order of Service Comparisons

By integrating the Taize format with a shorter order of service of the Episcopal church, an alternative Contemplative Worship Service could look like this:

A Contemplative Worship Service in the Christian Taize Tradition

5:00 PM
45–55 minutes:

A place to come as you are
To rest in God

In the album *Jesus Remember Me* by the London Fox Taize Choir are the following songs. Many of these are well-known.

Our Father (Lord's Prayer)
Be Still
Come Holy Spirit
Jesus Remember Me
O Lord, Hear My Prayer
Lamb of God
Wait for the Lord
Bless the Lord, My Soul
Ubi Caritas
Hearken My Voice
Laudate Luminum
Eat this Bread
Be Not Afraid

Hosanna in the Highest
In God Alone
Kyrie Eleison

This service is patterned after worship in the ecumenical community of Taizé. Their sung and silent participatory prayer services are designed for contemplation through music, song and silence. The brothers of Taizé explain, "Short chants, repeated again and again, give it a meditative character. Using just a few words, they express a basic reality of faith, quickly grasped by the mind. As the words are sung over many times, this reality gradually penetrates the whole being." Scripture is read slowly, candles and icons are to enhance Contemplative Worship. The different tempo of the Taizé service encourages us to break away from the hurried sense of our lives and breathe in the presence of Christ and community. (Calvin College, worship@ calvin.edu.)

Order of Service

- **A welcome** and introduction for newcomers to Contemplative Worship (Optional).

Play "Come Holy Spirit" (Taize song).

- **A gathering** in Silence around lighting of candles (labyrinth, or church).

- **A prayer of praise, thanks or guidance.**

Psalm 103. All speak together.

Praise the LORD, O my soul; all my inmost being, praise his holy name. Praise the LORD, O my soul, and forget not all his benefits, who forgives all your sins and heals all your diseases, who redeems your life from the pit and crowns you with love and compassion, who satisfies your desires with good things so that your youth is renewed like the eagle's. The LORD works righteousness and justice for all the oppressed.

Psalm 62:5–10 (NIV)

Yes, my soul, find rest in God; my hope comes from him. Truly he is my rock and my salvation; he is my fortress, I will not be shaken. My salvation and my honor depend on God; he is my mighty rock, my refuge. Trust in him at all times, you people; pour out your hearts to him, for God is our refuge.

Play and/or sing "Bless the Lord, My Soul" (Taize song).

- **A reading from Scripture.**

I John 2:7-11 (NIV) Mini homily (one paragraph)
Quote: Rev. John Piper, founder at desiringgod.org:

The beam of light that shines out from God through Jesus and through us into the world is the beam of love. One day this light will cover this earth like the water covers the sea. But for now it has already begun to shine in Jesus and in those "who walked the way he walked (2:6). To the degree that the gospel makes headway in the world and transforms people into those who love like Jesus, to that degree the darkness is passing away and the true light is already shining.

Read together verses below:

I John 4:7 (NIV)

Beloved, let us love one another, for love is from God, and whoever loves has been born of God and knows God. Anyone who does not love does not know God, because God is love.

John 8:12

When Jesus spoke again to the people, he said, "I am the light of the world. Whoever follows me will never walk in darkness, but will have the light of life."

Matthew 5:14–16

You are the light of the world. A town built on a hill cannot be hidden. Neither do people light a lamp and put it under a bowl. Instead they put it on its stand, and it gives light to everyone in the house. In the same way, let your light shine before others, that they may see your good deeds and glorify your Father in heaven.

- **Sing or play** "Be Still" or "Come Let Us Bow Down" (Taize songs).

- **A 10-, 15-, or 20-minute time of Silence and Reflection on Scripture** (lectio Divina)

- **An intercessory prayer for healing.**

Sing or play "Lord, Hear Our Prayer" (Taize song).

Prayers of Intercession, Ordinary 20, year A by Alison Holden at www.thisischurch.com. (The World Is Our Parish. Representing St. Marks & Putnoe Heights Churches (Bedford UK) by Rev Canon Royden & Friends):

Let us pray for all people [animals and plants, waters and seas] *in all parts of this troubled world, and in all kinds of need.*

Lord, shine your light upon those who live in danger of violence, persecution, oppression, displacement, loss and injustice because of race, belief, gender or who they are. We pray that the hearts of those who visit the evils of prejudice and greed upon others may be turned from darkness and awakened to the true light in the love and compassion of the Lord.

**Lord, in your mercy,
Hear our prayer.**

Lord, shine your light upon those who live in fear of famine, disease and destitution, and upon those who live without hope, faith or love, that they may know your true love and the joy of your salvation.

**Lord, in your mercy,
Hear our prayer.**

Lord, shine your light upon your church and all people of faith that their love may shine in the darkness, uniting in their endeavors for the common good. May we, in the ministries which are our lives, proclaim God's Love as our faith shines forth.

**Lord, in your mercy,
Hear our prayer.**

Lord, shine your light upon those who suffer in mind, body or spirit. Give them courage and hope in their troubles and bring them the joy of your redeeming love. We pray also for those who love and care for them. We name in our thoughts any known to us who are in special need of our prayers, in a moment of silence ...

**Lord, in your mercy,
Hear our prayer.**

Lord, shine your light upon those who mourn. Jesus Christ is the light of the world, a light which no darkness can quench. We remember before God those who have died and light a candle to symbolize the light of Christ, which eternally shines and brings hope. We remember ...

You turn our darkness into light: in your light shall we see light. Merciful Father, accept these prayers for the sake of your Son, our Savior Jesus Christ. Amen.

- **Lord's Prayer,** speak or sing "Our Father" (Taize song).

Gathering our prayers and praises into one, let us sing or say the **Lord's Prayer** *together:*

*Our Father who art in heaven, hallowed be thy name, thy kingdom come, thy will be done on earth as it is in heaven.
Give us this day our daily bread.
Forgive us our trespasses, as we forgive those who trespass against us.
And lead us not into temptation, but deliver us from evil.
For thine is the kingdom and the power and the glory forever. Amen.*

- **A time of re-gathering and breaking of bread** (pass in wooden bowl already broken and blest with blest cup of wine).

Read I Corinthians 11:23–26:

The Lord Jesus, on the night he was betrayed, took bread, and when he had given thanks, he broke it and said, "This is my body, which is for you; do this in remembrance of me." In the same way, after supper he took the cup, saying, "This cup is the new covenant in my blood; do this, whenever you drink it, in remembrance of me." For whenever you eat this bread and drink this cup, you proclaim the Lord's death until he comes.

People say as bread and cup are passed:

The body of Christ, the bread of heaven. Amen.
The blood of Christ, the cup of salvation. Amen.

Sing or play "Eat This Bread" (Taize song).

(Optional) Sing or play "Come, Drink of Living Water" (Taize song).

- **A benediction/blessing prayer.**

Sing or play "Jesus, Remember Me" (Taize song).

- **Dismissal in Silence.**

Optional: 6 PM. Light shared meal.

Chapter 4.

THE IONA ABBEY WORSHIP BOOK

What I like about the Iona pattern/order of worship for a Sunday morning is that it mirrors the Episcopal order of service, but uses fewer words. Their words are more in style with speech of the people. Iona also includes 20 minutes of Silence in their Quiet Services which are similar in pattern to the Taize service.

While not likely to be part of a Contemplative order of service, the affirmation of faith among different denominations illustrates how they differ in language relevance and degree of simplicity. For example, the Episcopal affirmation Of faith (Nicene Creed, English version) is:

We believe in one God,
the Father, the Almighty,

maker of heaven and earth,
of all that is, seen and unseen.

We believe in one Lord, Jesus Christ,
the only Son of God,
eternally begotten of the Father,
God from God, Light from Light,
true God from true God,
begotten, not made,
of one Being with the Father.

Through him all things were made.
For us and for our salvation
he came down from heaven:
by the power of the Holy Spirit
he became incarnate from the Virgin Mary,
and was made man.

For our sake he was crucified under Pontius Pilate;
he suffered death and was buried.
On the third day he rose again
in accordance with the Scriptures;
he ascended into heaven
and is seated at the right hand of the Father.
He will come again in glory to judge the living
and the dead,
and his kingdom will have no end.

We believe in the Holy Spirit, the Lord, the giver of life,
who proceeds from the Father and the Son.
With the Father and the Son he is worshiped and
glorified.
He has spoken through the Prophets.

We believe in one holy catholic and apostolic Church.
We acknowledge one baptism for the forgiveness of sins.
We look for the resurrection of the dead,
and the life of the world to come. Amen.

One affirmation of faith in the Iona Abbey Worship Book is simpler:

We believe in God above us,
Maker and Sustainer of all life,
of sun and moon,
of water and earth,
of male and female.

We believe in God beside us,
Jesus Christ, the Word made flesh,
born of a woman [blessed Mary],
servant of the poor,
tortured and nailed to a tree.

A man of compassion, he died forsaken;
he descended into the earth
to the place of death.

On the third day he rose from the tomb;
he ascended into heaven
to be everywhere present;
and his kingdom will come on earth.

We believe in God within us,
the Holy Spirit of Pentecostal fire,
life-giving breath of the church,
spirit of healing and forgiveness,
source of resurrection and eternal life. Amen.

Why not consider a version like this:

We believe in one God, all- powerful,
the Creator of life, sustainer of all creation;
We believe in God's incarnation on earth,
born from the womb of blessed Mary,

born human, made fully visible in his Son,
Jesus Christ, who revealed God's love
For creation entire;
who was then tortured and killed,
buried and resurrected,
then ascended into heaven.

We believe in God's Holy Spirit
Who ignites our souls to walk in Love and Light;
And that in loving God, others and creation entire,
and by God's mercy and grace,

*We enter God's realm of Love and Light,
whole and forgiven
now and forever. Amen.*

Easy to understand (I only share this as a comparison of styles) is the Modern Affirmation of Faith from the Williams Memorial CME (Christian Methodist Episcopal) Temple Church in Shreveport, Louisiana:

We believe in God the Father, infinite in wisdom, power and love, whose mercy is over all his works, and whose will is ever directed to his children's good.

We believe in Jesus Christ, Son of God and Son of man, the gift of the Father's unfailing grace, the ground of our hope, and the promise of our deliverance from sin and death.

We believe in the Holy Spirit as the divine presence in our lives, whereby we are kept in perpetual remembrance of the truth of Christ and find strength and help in time of need.

We believe that this faith should manifest itself in the service of love as set forth in the example of our blessed Lord, to the end that the kingdom of God may come upon the earth. Amen.

However, for the purpose of this book, which is to suggest simplifying liturgy specifically for alternate services for Contemplative Worship, I return to the *Iona Abbey Worship Book* for an outline of their Quiet Services which are similar in pattern to Taize worship but are without song:

The people gather
Opening prayer
Prayer
Silence 20 minutes
Prayer for others
Words of Sending/blessing

The full liturgy of Quiet Service 3A, and Quiet Service 3B and the appendix to services of Quiet 3C, which introduces participants to silent worship, can be found on pages 53-59 of the *Iona Abbey Worship Book*, copyright © 2017, WGRG, The Iona Community and can be obtained by permission from www.ionabooks.org at Wild Goose Publications.

Chapter 5.

SYNTHESIS OF WORSHIP PATTERNS

Why not incorporate the pattern and words of Iona's Quiet Services into "A Contemplative Worship Service in the Christian Taize Tradition"? It could look something like this:

**A Contemplative Worship Service
in the Christian Taize/Iona Tradition**

    5:00 PM
    45–55 minutes:

    A place to come as you are
    To rest in God

    This service is patterned after worship in the ecumenical community of Taizé. Their sung and silent participatory prayer services are designed for contemplation through music, song and silence. The brothers of Taizé explain, "Short chants, repeated again and again, give it a meditative character. Using just a few words, they express a basic reality of faith, quickly grasped by the mind. As the words are sung over many times, this reality gradually penetrates the whole being." Scripture is read slowly, candles and icons are to enhance Contemplative Worship. The different tempo of the Taizé service encourages us to break away from the hurried sense of our lives and breathe in the presence of Christ and community. (Calvin College, worship@calvin.edu)

Order of Service

- **A welcome** and introduction for newcomers to Contemplative Worship (Optional).

Play "Come, Holy Spirit" (Taize song).

- **A gathering** in Silence around lighting of candles (labyrinth, or church).

[Insert Opening prayer from Iona Quiet Service 3A].

Leader speaks:

Jesus,
You commanded waves to be still

and calmed a stormy sea.
Quiet now our restless hearts
that they may find rest in you.

We recognize the noise inside us
and the noises around us.
We acknowledge them,
but seek here to know your presence
in the midst of all that might distract us.

So, now we surrender for these moments our speech,
knowing that beneath the silence is a deeper word,
and that even when we say nothing,
you are still listening.

- **A prayer of praise, thanks, guidance.**

Psalm 103. All speak together:

Praise the LORD, O my soul; all my inmost being,
praise his holy name.
Praise the LORD, O my soul, and forget not all
his benefits,
who forgives all your sins and heals all your diseases,
who redeems your life from the pit and crowns you with
love and compassion,
who satisfies your desires with good things so that your
youth is renewed like the eagle's.

The LORD works righteousness and justice for all the oppressed.

Psalm 62:5–10 (NIV)

*Yes, my soul, find rest in God; my hope comes from him.
Truly he is my rock and my salvation; he is my fortress, I will not be shaken.
My salvation and my honor depend on God; he is my mighty rock, my refuge.
Trust in him at all times, you people; pour out your hearts to him, for God is our refuge.*

Play and/or sing "Bless the Lord, My Soul" (Taize song).

- **A reading from Scripture.**

I John 2:7-11 (NIV) Mini homily (one paragraph). Quote: Rev. John Piper, founder at desiringgod.org:

The beam of light that shines out from God through Jesus and through us into the world is the beam of love. One day this light will cover this earth like the water covers the sea. But for now it has already begun to shine in Jesus and in those "who walked the way he walked" (2:6). To the degree that the gospel makes headway in the world and transforms people into those who love like

Jesus, to that degree the darkness is passing away and the true light is already shining.

Read together verses below:

I John 4:7 (NIV)

Beloved, let us love one another, for love is from God, and whoever loves has been born of God and knows God. Anyone who does not love does not know God, because God is love.

John 8:12

When Jesus spoke again to the people, he said, "I am the light of the world. Whoever follows me will never walk in darkness, but will have the light of life."

Matthew 5:14–16

You are the light of the world. A town built on a hill cannot be hidden. Neither do people light a lamp and put it under a bowl. Instead they put it on its stand, and it gives light to everyone in the house. In the same way, let your light shine before others, that they may see your good deeds and glorify your Father in heaven.

- **Sing or play** "Be Still," "Come Let Us Bow Down," or "Our Soul Waits for the Lord" (Taize songs).

- **A 10-, 15-, or 20-minute time of Silence and Reflection on Scripture** (lectio Divina)

- **An intercessory prayer for healing.**

Sing or play "Lord, Hear Our Prayer" (Taize song).

From Prayers of Intercession, Ordinary 20, year A by Alison Holden at www.thisischurch.com.

Let us pray for all people [animals and plants, waters and seas] *in all parts of this troubled world, and in all kinds of need.*

Lord, shine your light upon those who live in danger of violence, persecution, oppression, displacement, loss and injustice because of race, belief, gender or who they are. We pray that the hearts of those who visit the evils of prejudice and greed upon others may be turned from darkness and awakened to the true light in the love and compassion of the Lord.

Lord, in your mercy,
Hear our prayer.

Lord, shine your light upon those who live in fear of famine, disease and destitution, and upon those who live without hope, faith or love, that they may know your true love and the joy of your salvation.

Lord, in your mercy,
Hear our prayer.

Lord, shine your light upon your church and all people of faith that their love may shine in the darkness, uniting in their endeavors for the common good. May we, in the ministries which are our lives, proclaim God's Love as our faith shines forth.

Lord, in your mercy,
Hear our prayer.

Lord, shine your light upon those who suffer in mind, body or spirit. Give them courage and hope in their troubles and bring them the joy of your redeeming love. We pray also for those who love and care for them. We name in our thoughts any known to us who are in special need of our prayers, in a moment of silence...

Lord, in your mercy,
Hear our prayer.

Lord, shine your light upon those who mourn. Jesus Christ is the light of the world, a light which no darkness can quench. We remember before God those who have died and light a candle to symbolize the light of Christ, which eternally shines and brings hope. We remember...

You turn our darkness into light: in your light shall we see light. Merciful Father, accept these prayers for the sake of your Son, our Savior Jesus Christ. Amen.

- **Lord's Prayer,** speak or sing "Our Father" (Taize song).

Gathering our prayers and praises into one, let us sing or say the **Lord's Prayer** *together:*

Our Father who art in heaven, hallowed be thy name, thy kingdom come, thy will be done on earth as it is in heaven.
Give us this day our daily bread.
Forgive us our trespasses, as we forgive those who trespass against us.
And lead us not into temptation, but deliver us from evil.
For thine is the kingdom and the power and the glory forever. Amen.

- **A time of re-gathering and breaking of bread** (pass in wooden bowl already broken and blest with blest cup of wine).

Read I Corinthians 11:23–26:

The Lord Jesus, on the night he was betrayed, took bread, and when he had given thanks, he broke it and said, "This is my body, which is for you; do this in remembrance of me." In the same way, after supper he took the cup, saying, "This cup is the new covenant in my blood; do this, whenever you drink it, in remembrance of me." For whenever you eat this bread and drink this cup, you proclaim the Lord's death until he comes.

People say as bread and cup are passed:

*The body of Christ, the bread of heaven. Amen.
The blood of Christ, the cup of salvation. Amen.*

Sing or play "Eat This Bread" (Taize song).

(Optional) Sing or play "Come, Drink of Living Water" (Taize song).

- **A benediction/blessing prayer.**

[Insert: Iona blessing from Quiet Service 3A]:

*May God be
a bright flame before you,
a guiding star above you,
a smooth path below you,
a kindly shepherd behind you,
[today]tonight and tomorrow and forever. Amen.*

Sing or play "Jesus, Remember Me" (Taize song).

- **Dismissal in Silence.**

Optional: 6 PM. Light shared meal.

Chapter 6.

CONCLUSION

My conclusion to offering these suggestions for an alternate Service of Contemplative Worship is this: people who are not served by traditional services of the main church of their denomination need alternative worship services, especially services that provide for Silence.

I believe alternative services must be provided by the main church. Otherwise, those who seek simple church outside the main church may go off the grid and their groups may not survive. The church must seek out their lost sheep and bring them home, making them feel welcomed and loved.

Subjects liturgy might focus on for alternate Contemplative Services are social justice, grief and loss, healing, or care of creation. Psalms, Old Testament Scripture readings, New Testament readings, and gospel readings along with prayer and songs for those services will fit the format I have provided in "A Contemplative Worship Service in the Christian Taize/Iona Tradition."

A creation-centered liturgy can be the focus of a service just by changing readings, prayers or songs, and even the introduction of a poem in place of all Scripture. For example, the following service adapts the format to become Creation inclusive:

A Contemplative Creation-Centered Worship Service in the Christian Taize/Iona Tradition

5:00 PM
45–55 minutes:

A place to come as you are
To rest in God

In the album *Jesus Remember Me* by the London Fox Taize Choir are the following songs, many you already know or know of:

Our Father (Lord's Prayer)
Be Still
Come Holy Spirit
Jesus, Remember Me
O Lord, Hear My Prayer
Lamb of God
Wait for the Lord

Bless the Lord, my Soul
Ubi Caritas
Hearken my Voice
Laudate Luminum
Eat this Bread
Be Not Afraid
Hosanna in the Highest
In God Alone
Kyrie Eleison

This service is patterned after worship in the ecumenical community of Taizé. Their sung and silent participatory prayer services are designed for contemplation through music, song and silence. The brothers of Taizé explain, "Short chants, repeated again and again, give it a meditative character. Using just a few words, they express a basic reality of faith, quickly grasped by the mind. As the words are sung over many times, this reality gradually penetrates the whole being." Scripture is read slowly, candles and icons are to enhance Contemplative Worship. The different tempo of the Taizé service encourages us to break away from the hurried sense of our lives and breathe in the presence of Christ and community. (Calvin College, worship@calvin.edu)

Order of Service

- **A welcome** and introduction for newcomers to Contemplative Worship.

Play "Come, Holy Spirit" (Taize song).

- **A gathering** in Silence around lighting of candles (labyrinth, chapel, outdoors).

[Insert Opening prayer from Iona Quiet Service 3A].

Leader speaks:

Jesus,
You commanded waves to be still
and calmed a stormy sea.
Quiet now our restless hearts
that they may find rest in you.

We recognize the noise inside us
and the noises around us.
We acknowledge them,
but seek here to know your presence
In the midst of all that might distract us.

So, now we surrender for these moments our speech,
knowing that beneath the silence is a deeper word,
and that even when we say nothing,
you are still listening.

- **A prayer of praise, thanks, guidance.**

Psalm 148

Praise the LORD from the heavens;
praise him in the heights above.
Praise him, all his angels;
praise him, all his heavenly hosts.
Praise him, sun and moon;
praise him, all you shining stars.
Praise him, you highest heavens
and you waters above the skies.

Let them praise the name of the LORD,
for at his command they were created,
and he established them for ever and ever—
he issued a decree that will never pass away.

Praise the LORD from the earth,
you great sea creatures and all ocean depths,
lightning and hail, snow and clouds,
stormy winds that do his bidding,
you mountains and all hills,
fruit trees and all cedars,
wild animals and all cattle,
small creatures and flying birds,
kings of the earth and all nations,
you princes and all rulers on earth,
young men and women,
old men and children.

Let them praise the name of the LORD,
for his name alone is exalted;
his splendor is above the earth and the heavens.

Thanksgivings for the Natural Order. *For the Beauty of the Earth*

BCP p. 840

We give you thanks, most gracious God, for the beauty of earth and sky and sea; for the richness of mountains, plains, and rivers; for the songs of birds and the loveliness of flowers. We praise you for these good gifts, and pray that we may safeguard them for our posterity. Grant that we may continue to grow in our grateful enjoyment of your abundant creation, to the honor and glory of your Name, now and forever. Amen.

BCP p. 836

Accept, O Lord, our thanks and praise for all that you have done for us. We thank you for the splendor of the whole creation, for the beauty of this world, for the wonder of life, and for the mystery of love.

- **A reading from Scripture.**

I John 2:7–11 (NIV) Mini homily (one paragraph). Quote: Rev. John Piper, founder at desiringgod.org:

> *The beam of light that shines out from God through Jesus and through us into the world is the beam of love. One day this light will cover this earth like the water covers the sea. But for now it has already begun to shine in Jesus and in those "who walked the way he walked" (2:6). To the degree that the gospel makes headway in the world and transforms people into those who love like Jesus, to that degree the darkness is passing away and the true light is already shining.*

Read together verses below:

I John 4:7 (NIV)
> *Beloved, let us love one another, for love is from God, and whoever loves has been born of God and knows God. Anyone who does not love does not know God, because God is love.*

John 8:12
> *When Jesus spoke again to the people, he said, "I am the light of the world. Whoever follows me will never walk in darkness, but will have the light of life."*

John 12:36
> *Believe in the light while you have the light, so that you may become children of light."*

Romans 8:19

For the creation waits in eager expectation for the children of [Light] God to be revealed.

- **Sing or play** "Be Still," "Come Let Us Bow Down," or "Our Soul Waits for the Lord" (Taize songs).

- **A 10- to 20-minute time of Silence and Reflection on Scripture** (lectio Divina)

- **An intercessory prayer for healing.**

Sing or play "Lord, Hear Our Prayer" (Taize song).

From Prayers of Intercession, Ordinary 20, year A by Alison Holden at www.thisischurch.com.

Let us pray for all people [animals and plants, waters and seas] *in all parts of this troubled world, and in all kinds of need.*

Lord, shine your light upon those who live in danger of violence, persecution, oppression, displacement, loss and injustice because of race, belief, gender or who they are. We pray that the hearts of those who visit the evils of prejudice and greed upon others may be turned from darkness and awakened to the true light in the love and compassion of the Lord.

**Lord, in your mercy,
Hear our prayer.**

Lord, shine your light upon those who live in fear of famine, disease and destitution, and upon those who live without hope, faith or love, that they may know your true love and the joy of your salvation.

**Lord, in your mercy,
Hear our prayer.**

Lord, shine your light upon your church and all people of faith that their love may shine in the darkness, uniting in their endeavors for the common good. May we, in the ministries which are our lives, proclaim God's Love as our faith shines forth.

**Lord, in your mercy,
Hear our prayer.**

Lord, shine your light upon those who suffer in mind, body or spirit. Give them courage and hope in their troubles and bring them the joy of your redeeming love. We pray also for those who love and care for them. We name in our thoughts any known to us who are in special need of our prayers, in a moment of silence...

**Lord, in your mercy,
Hear our prayer.**

> *Lord, shine your light upon those who mourn. Jesus Christ is the light of the world, a light which no darkness can quench. We remember before God those who have died and light a candle to symbolize the light of Christ, which eternally shines and brings hope. We remember...*
>
> *You turn our darkness into light: in your light shall we see light. Merciful Father, accept these prayers for the sake of your Son, our Savior Jesus Christ. Amen.*

- **Lord's Prayer,** say or sing together or play "Our Father" (Taize song).

Gathering our prayers and praises into one, let us sing or say the **Lord's Prayer** together:

Our Father who art in heaven, hallowed be thy name, thy kingdom come, thy will be done on earth as it is in heaven.
Give us this day our daily bread.
Forgive us our trespasses, as we forgive those who trespass against us.
And lead us not into temptation, but deliver us from evil.
For thine is the kingdom and the power and the glory forever. Amen.

- **A time of re-gathering and breaking of bread** (pass in wooden bowl already broken and blest with blest cup of wine).

Read I Corinthians 11:23–26:

The Lord Jesus, on the night he was betrayed, took bread, and when he had given thanks, he broke it and said, "This is my body, which is for you; do this in remembrance of me." In the same way, after supper he took the cup, saying, "This cup is the new covenant in my blood; do this, whenever you drink it, in remembrance of me." For whenever you eat this bread and drink this cup, you proclaim the Lord's death until he comes.

People say as bread and cup are passed:

*The body of Christ, the bread of heaven. Amen.
The blood of Christ, the cup of salvation. Amen.*

Sing or play "Eat This Bread" (Taize song).

(Optional) Sing or play "Come, Drink of the Living Water" (Taize song).

- **A benediction/blessing prayer.**

[Insert: Iona blessing from Quiet Service 3A]:

*May God be
a bright flame before you,
a guiding star above you,
a smooth path below you,
a kindly shepherd behind you,
[today]tonight and tomorrow and forever. Amen.*

Sing and play "Jesus, Remember Me" (Taize song).

- **Dismissal in Silence.**

Optional: 6 PM. Light shared meal.

An additional resource for the creation-centered service could be this poem, "Pied Beauty" by Gerald Manley Hopkins, incorporated in the praise section of the order of service:

*Glory be to God for dappled things—
For skies of couple-colour as a brinded cow;
For rose-moles all in stipple upon trout that swim;
Fresh-firecoal chestnut-falls; finches' wings;
Landscape plotted and pieced—fold, fallow,
and plough;
And all trades, their gear and tackle and trim.
All things counter, original, spare, strange;
Whatever is fickle, freckled (who knows how?)
With swift, slow; sweet, sour; adazzle, dim;*

He fathers-forth whose beauty is past change:
Praise Him.

Why not use poems if they are in keeping with the simpler liturgy for a Contemplative Service?

Consider also use of familiar hymns that are not Taize, which are found in our own hymnals. For example, in the Friends hymnal *Worship In Song*, the hymn "Spirit of the Living God" might be used in the order of service rather than a Taize chant. Or the hymn "Spirit of God Descend Upon my Heart" could be sung. In the creation-centered liturgy above, why not incorporate hymns such as "For the Beauty of the Earth" or "God of all Creation"?

There are many hymns that might fit a simplified liturgy other than Taize. The tempo, theme, or mood of the Contemplative Service will determine choice of songs, prayers, poems, and Old and New Testament and gospel readings.

My point is, as long as the theology is good, why not enliven our liturgies, specifically Contemplative Worship Services, with imagery, words and songs that stick in the mind and heart. Candles, bells, or simple instruments all work to enhance liturgy.

To all creative worship planners, music directors, and everyone else whose job is to provide a meaningful worship experience, challenge your main churches to simplify tired liturgy.

My heart is intent on bringing this message to those who care about those who leave the church, the ones who no longer feel connected to God in church and are looking for other ways to find that connection.

I believe that the church must draw them back in with simplified liturgy for Contemplative Worship, preferably in simple, natural settings, a labyrinth or candlelit chapel.

Afterword

CREATING AN ONLINE ORDER OF SERVICE FOR CONTEMPLATIVE WORSHIP

Enter the Virtual Church which evolved out of the Coronavirus pandemic of 2020 as churches all over the world closed down. A whole new way of worship opened up for those lost sheep who had strayed from the main church or who were not able to attend physically.

Remember that the lost sheep are not the ones showing up in physical church buildings every Sunday morning. They are scattered all over the world, some hidden away, others too infirm to travel to attend church, still others who are isolated by fear. All craving to be loved and to know a God who loves them unconditionally.

The coronavirus pandemic closed down the churches along with everything else and people had to stay home to prevent the spread of it. Churches quickly, and some awkwardly, had to adjust to stream services online to satisfy their Sunday morning congregations. Virtual church was born out of the necessity to reach isolated congregants and is here to stay.

What connects us to the church now, since the coronavirus pandemic of 2020 that shut us in for several months, is the digital age. Not since the invention of the printing press, that changed how we receive information, has the human family connected more universally via I Phones, Tablets and I Pads, Computers, YouTube videos, Instagram, Twitter and Zoom channels.

For a while we have seen people sitting across from one another communicating by phone and thought it silly! Now with social distancing restrictions it may be the new normal!

The digital age is the new normal for many, even as we resume attending church in person, go out shopping, dining and gathering socially. But will the brick and mortar church survive the new normal with in person attendance at an all-time low yet with dramatic increases in attendance with online viewing?

According to a June 4th 2020 blog by Gene Veith, titled, *The Newest Church Growth Paradigm: Digital Church,* Veith says that,

"The [coronavirus] epidemic [of 2020] has forced churches to resort to online services. But now some church growth experts are hailing that problem as a new paradigm for "doing church." Church growth expert, Carey Nieuwhof, also advocates "digital" church...

In his post **The Original 2020 is History**... Rev. Nieuwhof sees "digital church," rather than just "physical church" as the wave of the future. Digital technology, he says, will accelerate the trend we are already seeing in the "consolidation" of the church, as smaller congregations close in favor of fewer but bigger megachurches. And yet, Rev. Nieuwhof says,

"The physical churches will not disappear... Growing churches in the future will become digital organizations with physical expressions, not physical organizations with a digital presence... Online church transcends geographic, physical and time barriers in a way that analog doesn't...Will we still have in-person, physical gatherings and services? Absolutely. But in the future church, if you care about people, you'll care about digital church."

Topics for Worship

Wow! I love the digital age because I am a digital artist. As a graduate of Divinity School, with a Master of Arts in Religion, digital ministry is the calling I never expected. But here we are.

In the Appendix, I am adding scripts for under 20-minute YouTube Contemplative Worship Services which are shorter versions of the order of service provided in this book. **Links to the videos are available on my website at www.**

ContemplativeWorshipOnline.com. Click on the menu bars then click on 'Services'.

Topics for worship include a Lenten Service, a Grief and Loss Service, a Healing Service, a Service of Thanksgiving, a Service Remembering those who have Died, a shortened Creation-centered Service, a Service for Justice and Peace, and yes, even a Service Remembering the Holy Eucharist usually administered by the ordained!

I feel sure worship leaders will be led by the Holy Spirit in this time of digitally modernizing the main church. I believe this is Holy and creative work, and the church will grow with the new technology. I am grateful to be at the leading edge of this new ministry.

I recommend visiting the following websites of church leaders discussing the future of the church online: Dr. Diana Butler Bass, The Reverend Joshua Case, The Very Rev Kelvin Holdsworth, and Dr. Deanna A. Thompson.

See their You Tube video, "Being the Church in This Time of Pandemic," May 19, 2020, which inspired me to create an online service, Remembering the Holy Eucharist, that would normally be done by an ordained person of the church.

Also, visit the blog site of church growth expert, Rev. Carey Nieuwhof at Carey Nieuwhof.com.

APPENDIX

Scripts for Contemplative Worship YouTube videos, each one under 20-minutes.

I. a Lenten Service, **II.** a Grief and Loss Service, **III.** a Service Remembering those who have Died, **IV.** a Healing Service, **V.** a Service of Thanksgiving, **VI.** a Service Remembering the Holy Eucharist, **VII.** a shortened Creation-centered Service, **VIII.** a Service for Justice and Peace

I. Contemplative Worship Lenten Service

Opening

Come let us rest for a while in the presence of God in the sacred sanctuary of our home.

Let us worship together in Silence, with songs from the Taizé community in France, sung by the London Fox Taizé Choir, prayers from the Iona community in Scotland, and Scripture from the New and Old Testaments.

By resting in God may you find peace and well-being in this Contemplative service. In Christ we gather [although remotely] to worship our Lord. Amen.

Taizé song: *Come Let Us Bow Down*, Come on bended knee. Kneel before the Lord, our Maker.

Reading: Psalm 62: 5-10 (NIV)

Yes, my soul, find rest in God; my hope comes from him. Truly he is my rock and my salvation; he is my fortress; I will not be shaken. My salvation and my honor depend on God; he is my mighty rock, my refuge. Trust in him at all times, you people, pour out you hearts to him, for God is our refuge.

Silence

Taizé song: *In God Alone* my soul can find rest and peace. In God my peace and joy. Only in God can my soul find her rest, find her rest and peace.

Appendix

Reading: 1 John 4:7 (NIV)

Beloved, let us love one another, for love is from God. Whoever loves has been born of God and knows God. Anyone who does not love, does not know God, because God is Love.

Silence.

Taizé song: *Ubi Caritas* et Amor, Ubi caritas, Deus ibi est. [Live in charity and steadfast love. Live in charity, God will dwell with you.]

Reading: *Lord's Prayer*: Our Father who art in heaven, hallowed be thy name. Thy kingdom come, thy will be done, on earth as it is in heaven. Give us this day our daily bread and forgive us our trespasses as we forgive those who have trespassed against us. And lead us not into temptation but deliver us from evil. For thine is kingdom and the power and the glory for ever and ever. Amen.

Taizé song: *In the Lord I'll be Ever Thankful,* in the Lord I will rejoice. Look to God, do not be afraid. Lift up your voices the Lord is near. Lift up your voices the Lord is near.

Closing: May God bless you, protect you and heal you. Go in peace to love and serve the Lord. Amen.

II. Grief and Loss Contemplative Worship Service

Taizé Song: Be Still

Come, be still and rest awhile in the presence of God. In your grief and loss, may you find comfort and peace in this time apart to worship our Lord who stands beside you.

You are listening to songs from the Taizé community in France, sung by the London Fox Taizé Choir.

***Opening prayer, For Quiet Confidence*, From the Book of Common Prayer.**

O God of peace, *who hast* taught us that in returning and rest we shall be saved, in quietness and confidence shall be our strength: By the might of *thy* Spirit lift us, we pray *thee*, to *thy* presence, where we may be still and know that *thou art* God; through Jesus Christ our Lord. *Amen.*

Taizé Song: Come Holy Spirit

Let us pray,

Lord, we turn to You in our brokenness and grief seeking your solace and grace. We suffer agonizing pain from loss, anger and anxiety for our future.

Appendix

Comfort us as we take refuge in you, apart from caring loved ones, concerned acquaintances and the distractions of disquieting thoughts. Heal our broken hearts with a deeper peace than we have ever known. Mercifully restore our brokenness to wholeness with a new heart for living according to your purpose. Amen.

Taizé song: The Lord is Gracious

Our first Scripture readings are from the OT, Psalm 130:1-2 (NIV) **Psalm** 34:18,22 and **Jerimiah** 29:11:

Psalm 130: 1-2 Out of the depths I cry to you, LORD. Lord, hear my voice. Let your ears be attentive to my cry…

Psalm 34:18,22

The LORD is close to the brokenheartedand saves those who are crushed in spirit. The LORD will rescue his servants… who takes refuge in him.

Jeremiah 29:11 For I know the plans I have for you," declares the Lord, "plans to prosper you and not to harm you, plans to give you hope and a future.

Our second reading is from the N.T., Romans 8:35-38

Who shall separate us from the love of Christ? Shall trouble or hardship or persecution or famine or nakedness or danger or sword? As it is written:

"For your sake we face death all day long: we are considered as sheep to be slaughtered." No, in all these things we are more than conquerors through him who loved us. For I am convinced that neither death nor life, neither angels nor demons, neither the present nor the future, nor any powers, neither height nor depth, nor anything else in all creation, will be able to separate us from the love of God that is in Christ Jesus our Lord."

Our last readings are from the NT, Philippians 4: 5-7 and 1 Peter 5:10-11

The Lord is near.

Do not be anxious about anything, but in every situation, by prayer and petition, with thanksgiving, present your requests to God.

And the peace of God, which transcends all understanding, will guard your hearts and your minds in Christ Jesus.

1 Peter 5:10-11

And the God of all grace, who called you to his eternal glory in Christ, after you have suffered a little while, will himself restore you and make you strong, firm and steadfast. To him be the power for ever and ever. Amen.

Appendix

Let us take a few moments of Silence

Let us pray together in silence as we listen to the Lord's Prayer sung by the London Fox Taizé choir.

We close with a prayer for guidance from the Book of Common Prayer

O God, ...Grant us, in all our doubts and uncertainties, the grace to ask what *thou would* have us to do, that the Spirit of wisdom may save us from all false choices, and that in *thy* light we may see light, and in *thy* straight path may not stumble; through Jesus Christ our Lord. *Amen.*

May the Lord Bless you and guide you today, tomorrow and in all the days ahead. Go in peace to love and serve the Lord and your neighbors as yourselves.

Taizé song: In the Lord I will be Thankful

III. Contemplative Service Remembering the Deceased

Come, be still and rest awhile in the presence of God. May you find comfort and peace in this time apart to remember our loved one(s) who have died.

You are listening to a Contemplative Service of Remembrance with songs from the Taizé community in France, sung by the London Fox Taizé Choir, with Scripture readings from the Old and New Testaments of the NIV bible, and prayers from the Anglican Diocese of Gloucester.

Taizé song. Jesus Remember Me

Opening Prayer: From the Anglican Diocese of Gloucester

15. God of mercy, Lord of life, you have made us in your image to reflect your truth and light: we give you thanks for those whom we remember today for the grace and mercy they received from you, for all that was good in their lives, for the memories we treasure today. We thank you for all who through your grace have lived according to your will and are now at rest. May their good example encourage and guide us all the days of our life. Meet us in our sadness and fill our hearts with praise and thanksgiving. Amen.

OT Reading Psalm 139:7-10 NIV

Where can I go from your Spirit? Where can I flee from your presence? If I go up to the heavens, you are there; if I make my bed in the depths, you are there. If I rise on the wings of the dawn, if I settle on the far side of the sea, even there your hand will guide me, your right hand will hold me fast.

NT Reading: Romans 8:38-39 NIV

For I am convinced that neither death nor life, neither angels nor demons, neither the present nor the future, nor any powers, neither height nor depth, nor anything else in all creation, will be able to separate us from the love of God that is in Christ Jesus our Lord.

Taizé song: Bless the Lord My Soul

Silence: Let us take a few moments of silence to remember fondly our loved ones who have died with memories most dear to us. May we forgive them their worst times, where necessary, and thank them for their best.

Taizé song: Lord's Prayer. Let us silently say the Lord's Prayer as we listen to the London Fox Taizé Choir.

Closing:

May God give to you and to all those whom you love his comfort and his peace, his light and his joy, in this world and the next; and the blessing of God almighty, the Father, the Son, and the Holy Spirit, be upon you and remain with you always. Amen.

Taizé song; In God Alone

IV. A Contemplative Worship Service for Healing

Come, be still and rest awhile in the presence of God. May you find comfort and peace in this time apart to worship our Lord.

You are listening to a service for healing with songs from the Taizé community in France, sung by the London Fox Taizé Choir with Scripture readings from the Old and New Testaments of the NIV bible.

Taizé song: Kyrie Eleison

Opening prayer

Lord, we ask you, in this time apart in word and prayer, to be attentive to our cry for a return to health and wholeness of Spirit that only a deeper communion with you supplies. May your grace fill us with knowing all shall be well according to your will. And if we should die, that you will bring us home into your loving arms where we will remain with you and our loved ones forever. Amen.

Taizé song: O Lord hear my prayer

Our first readings are from the OT. Psalm 6:2, Jeremiah 17:14 and Isaiah 33:2.

Jeremiah 17:14 "Heal me, O Lord, and I will be healed; save me and I will be saved, for you are the one I praise."

Psalms 6:2 "Have mercy on me, LORD, for I am faint; heal me, LORD, for my bones are in agony."

Isaiah 33:2 "LORD, be gracious to us; we long for you. Be our strength every morning, our salvation in time of distress."

Our second readings are from the NT. I Corinthians 10:13 and Jeremiah 29:11-13.

1 Corinthians 10:13 "Come to me, all you who are weary and burdened, and I will give you rest. Take my yoke upon you and learn from me, for I am gentle and humble in heart..." No temptation has overtaken you except what is common to mankind. And God is faithful; he will not let you be tempted beyond what you can bear. But when you are tempted, he will also provide a way out so that you can endure it."

James 5:6 "Therefore, confess your sins to each other and pray for each other so that you may be healed. The prayer of a righteous person is powerful and effective."

Jeremiah 29:11-13

For I know the plans I have for you," declares the Lord, "plans to prosper you and not to harm you, plans to give you hope and a future. Then you will call on me and come and pray to me, and I will listen to you. You will seek me and find me when you seek me with all your heart.

Let us take a few moments of Silence for private prayers.

Let us pray for ourselves, our families and friends and all people—animals and plants, waters and seas] in all parts of this troubled world, and in all kinds of need.

Taizé song: The Lord is Gracious

Our last Scripture readings are from Isaiah 41:10 and Jeremiah 30:17 and Psalms 73:26 and 103:2-4.

Isaiah 41:10 "So do not fear, for I am with you; do not be dismayed, for I am your God. I will strengthen you and help you; I will uphold you with my righteous right hand."

Jeremiah 30:17 "I will restore you to health and heal your wounds,' declares the LORD"

Psalms 73:26 "My flesh and my heart may fail, but God is the strength of my heart and my portion forever."

Psalms 103:2-4 "Praise the LORD, my soul, and forget not all his benefits - who forgives all your sins and heals all your diseases, who redeems your life from the pit and crowns you with love and compassion."

Taizé song. Lord's Prayer. Let us listen to the LP sung by the London Fox Taizé Choir

Closing prayer

NT John 14:27 "Peace I leave with you; my peace I give you. I do not give to you as the world gives. Do not let your hearts be troubled and do not be afraid."

Taizé song: Lord hear my prayer

V. A Contemplative Worship Service of Thanksgiving

Taizé song: In the Lord I will be Thankful

Come, be still and rest awhile in the presence of God. May you find comfort and peace in this time apart to worship our Lord.

You are listening to a service of Thanksgiving with songs from the Taizé community in France, sung by the London Fox Taizé Choir with Scripture readings from the Old and New Testaments of the NIV bible.

Psalm 99:9. Exalt the LORD our God and worship at his holy mountain, for the LORD our God is holy.

Opening Prayer

Lord, we are most thankful to you for leading us safely through this time of trial and upheaval and for being with us during our suffering and grief as well as during periods of creativity and joy. We thank you, especially, for the opportunity to learn new ways to connect with one another. May we continue, to be charitable and compassionate toward one another as we share our common bond in times of adversity. In Christ, our Lord, Amen.

Our first readings are from the OT Psalm 118:14-29 and Psalm 100 (NIV)

The Lord is my strength and my defense; he has become my salvation.

Shouts of joy and victory resound in the tents of the righteous: The Lord's right hand has done mighty things! The Lord's right hand is lifted high; the Lord's right hand has done mighty things!"

I will not die but live, and will proclaim what the Lord has done. The Lord has chastened me severely, but he has not given me over to death.

Open for me the gates of the righteous; I will enter and give thanks to the Lord.

Psalm 100: 1-5. Shout for joy to the LORD, all the earth. Worship the LORD with gladness; come before him with joyful songs. Know that the LORD is God. It is he who made us, and we are his; we are his people, the sheep of his pasture. Enter his gates with thanksgiving and his courts with praise; give thanks to him and praise his name. For the LORD is good and his love endures forever; his faithfulness continues through all generations.

Psalm 7:17. "I will give to the Lord the thanks due to his righteousness, and I will sing praise to the name of the Lord, the Most High."

Taizé song; Bless the Lord

Our second readings are from the New Testament, Colossians, and Philippians

Col. 2:7. "Let your roots grow down into him, and let your lives be built on him. Then your faith will grow strong in the truth you were taught, and you will overflow with thankfulness."

Col. 4:2. "Devote yourselves to prayer, being watchful and thankful."

Phil 4:6. "Do not be anxious about anything, but in everything by prayer and supplication with thanksgiving let your requests be made known to God."

Let us take a few moments of Silence for private prayers.

Let us thank God for our well-being, and the well-being of our families and friends and for the uniting of the world as we come together to praise and thank him for his steadfast love and mercy.

Taizé song: **Lord's Prayer**. Let us listen to the LP sung by the London Fox Taizé Choir

Closing Prayer:

Col. 3:15 "And let the peace of Christ rule in your hearts, to which indeed you were called in one body; and be thankful."

Taizé song: Sing, Praise and bless the Lord

VI. Remembering the Holy Eucharist II.

REVISED 6/2/2020

A Contemplative Service of reflection on the Lord's supper

Come, be still and rest awhile in the presence of God. May you find comfort and peace in this time apart to worship our Lord.

Taizé song. Be Still

You are listening to a Contemplative Service of reflection on the Lord's supper or the Holy Eucharist, usually administered by a priest or a deacon. A longer traditional version can be found in the Book of Common Prayer known as the Great Thanksgiving. You are hearing songs from the Taizé community in France, sung by the London Fox Taizé Choir,

Opening prayer

Lord, we gather here at your table to remember the meaning of the holy Eucharist, the sharing of your body and blood sacrificed for us by your death and resurrection. Be present with us now as we gaze upon these elements of bread and wine. Fill us with your loving spirit and heal us of our infirmities of body, mind and soul, so that we may go into the world prepared by renewal of your presence in us and through us to love and serve others with thankful hearts.. Amen.

Taizé song: Veni Sanctus Spiritus

Scripture readings from gospel of John 6:35 and Luke 22:7-38.

John 6:35

Then Jesus declared, "I am the bread of life. Whoever comes to me will never go hungry, and whoever believes in me will never be thirsty."

The story of the Lord' Supper is told in the gospels: This is a reading from the gospel of **Luke 22:7-38**.

The Last Supper

Then came the day of Unleavened Bread on which the Passover lamb had to be sacrificed. Jesus sent Peter and John, saying, "Go and make preparations for us to eat the Passover."

"Where do you want us to prepare for it?" they asked.

He replied, "As you enter the city, a man carrying a jar of water will meet you. Follow him to the house that he enters, and say to the owner of the house, 'The Teacher asks: Where is the guest room, where I may eat the Passover with my disciples?' He will show you a large room upstairs, all furnished. Make preparations there."

They left and found things just as Jesus had told them. So they prepared the Passover.

When the hour came [on the night Jesus was betrayed], Jesus and his apostles reclined at the table. And he said to them, "I have eagerly desired to eat this Passover with you before I suffer. For I tell you, I will not eat it again until it finds fulfillment in the kingdom of God."

After taking the cup, he gave thanks and said, "Take this and divide it among you. For I tell you I will not drink again from the fruit of the vine until the kingdom of God comes."

And he took bread, gave thanks and broke it, and gave it to them, saying, "This is my body given for you; do this in remembrance of me."

In the same way, after the supper he took the cup, saying, "This cup is the new covenant in my blood, which is poured out for you."

Taizé song: Lamb of God

Let us take a few moments of Silence to rest in the Lord's Presence remembering his death and resurrection.

Silently, say The Lord's Prayer as it is sung by the London Fox Taizé Choir.

Blessing

Lord, in this sacred time apart with you, you have searched our hearts and know our needs, Fortify us with spiritual food and drink by your Holy Spirit so that we might bring your grace and compassion into the world, though our corner of it may be small. Let us go forth in peace and love to serve you according to your will, with gratitude and joy. Amen.

Taize song: Eat this Bread

VII. A Contemplative Creation-Centered Worship Service

Come, be still and rest awhile in the presence of God. May you find comfort and peace in this time apart to worship our Lord.

Taizé song: Be Still

You are listening to a Creation- centered Service with songs from the Taizé community in France, sung by the London Fox Taizé Choir. Readings from the Book of Common Prayer and scripture from the Old and New Testaments, with prayers from the Iona community in Scotland.

BCP p. 836. Accept, O Lord, our thanks and praise for all that you have done for us. We thank you for the splendor of the whole creation, for the beauty of this world, for the wonder of life, and for the mystery of love.

Our Opening prayer is from the Quiet Service of the Iona community

Jesus, You commanded waves to be still and calmed a stormy sea. Quiet now our restless hearts that they may find rest in you.

We recognize the noise inside us and the noises around us. We acknowledge them, but seek here to know your presence In the midst of all that might distract us. So, now we surrender for these moments our speech, knowing that beneath the silence is a deeper word, and that even when we say nothing, you are still listening.

Taizé song: In God Alone

A reading from Psalm 148 of the OT. "Praise the Lord from the heavens; praise him in the heights above. Praise him, all his angels; praise him, all his heavenly hosts. Praise him, sun and moon; praise him, all you shining stars. Praise him, you highest heavens and you waters above the skies."

"Praise the Lord from the earth, you great sea creatures and all ocean depths, lightning and hail, snow and clouds, stormy winds that do his bidding, you mountains and all hills, fruit trees and all cedars, wild animals and all cattle, small creatures and flying birds, kings of the earth and all nations, you princes and all rulers on earth, young men and women, old men and children."

"Let them praise the name of the Lord, for his name alone is exalted; his splendor is above the earth and the heaven."

Taizé song. In the Lord I'll be Ever Thankful

Let us give Thanks for the Natural Order. *For the Beauty of the Earth*

BCP p. 840. We give you thanks, most gracious God, for the beauty of earth and sky and sea; for the richness of mountains, plains, and rivers; for the songs of birds and the loveliness of flowers. We praise you for these good gifts and pray that we may safeguard them for our posterity. Grant that we may continue to grow in our grateful enjoyment of your abundant creation, to the honor and glory of your Name, now and forever. Amen.

Readings from NT Scripture.

I John 4:7 (NIV) Beloved, let us love one another, for love is from God, and whoever loves has been born of God and knows God. Anyone who does not love does not know God, because God is love.

Romans 8:19 For the creation waits in eager expectation for the children of God to be revealed.

Take a few moments for Silent Prayer

In silence, let us pray for all people [animals and plants, waters and seas] in all parts of this troubled world, and in all kinds of need. May we remember that we are the caretakers of God's creation and that the earth's healing begins with us.

Taizé song: The Lord is Gracious

And now let us together say the Lord's Prayer. "Our Father, who art in Heaven…

Closing

We end with a blessing from Iona's Quiet Service 3A:

May God be a bright flame before you, a guiding star above you, a smooth path below you, a kindly shepherd behind you, [today]tonight and tomorrow and forever. Amen.

Go in peace to love and serve the Lord and his Creation entire.

Appendix

VII. A Contemplative Worship Service for Justice

Taizé song: Kyrie Eleison

Come let us rest for a while in the presence of God. By resting in God may you find peace and well-being in this Contemplative worship service,

In Christ we gather [remotely] to worship our Lord, seeking his guidance and mercy during this time of social unrest.

You are listening to songs from the Taize community in France with sung prayer by the London Fox Taizé Choir, Scripture readings from the Old and New Testament and prayers from the BCP and Iona Community's Act of Commitment.

OPENING PRAYER is from the BCP 27 and 28.

Prayers for the Social Order *28. In Times of Conflict and Social injustice:* O God, you have bound us together in a common life. Help us, in the midst of our struggles for justice and truth, to confront one another without hatred or bitterness, and to work together with mutual forbearance and respect.

Grant, O God, that your holy and life-giving Spirit may so move every human heart [and especially the hearts of the people of this land], that barriers which divide us may crumble, suspicions disappear, and hatreds cease; that our divisions being healed, we may live in justice and peace; through Jesus Christ our Lord. *Amen.*

NT Scripture Reading: 1 John 4:7 (NIV)

Beloved, let us love one another, for love is from God. Whoever loves has been born of God and knows God. Anyone who does not love, does not know God, because God is Love.

Taizé Song: *Ubi Caritas* et Amor. Ubi caritas, Deus ibi est. [Live in charity and steadfast love. Live in charity, God will dwell with you.]

Silence

Prayer from the BCP, 3. For the Human Family O God, you made us in your own image and redeemed us through Jesus your Son: Look with compassion on the whole human family; take away the arrogance and hatred which infect our hearts; break down the walls that separate us; unite us in bonds of love; and work through our struggle and confusion to accomplish your purposes on earth; that, in your good time, all nations and races may serve you in harmony, through Jesus Christ our Lord. *Amen.*

OT Scripture reading, Micah 6:8:

He has shown you, O mortal, what is good. And what does the LORD require of you? To act justly and to love mercy and to walk humbly with your God.

Lord's Prayer sung by the London Fox Taizé Choir

Closing

PRAYER OF COMMITMENT from the Act of Commitment A 3, IONA COMMUNITY

In gratitude for this moment, this place, those around us, Christ among us, we give ourselves to you our God. Take us out to live as changed people because we have met the risen Christ and cannot be the same.

Ask much of us, expect much from us, enable much by us, encourage many through us. So that we may we live to your glory both as inhabitants of earth and citizens of the commonwealth of heaven. Amen.

Taizé song: In God Alone

Benediction

Go forward in love as people changed by Christ to be a new creation, one serving all of creation both human and non, with concern for justice and peace. Amen.

CITED WORKS

Foreword
What is Taize? See also the Taize website at www.taize.fr.

What is Iona? From the website of the New World Foundation at: http://iona-nwf.org/the-iona-community/:

"The Iona Community, founded in 1938 by the Rev George MacLeod, then a parish minister in Glasgow, Scotland, is an ecumenical Christian community that is committed to seeking new ways of living the Gospel in today's world. Initially this purpose was expressed through the rebuilding of the monastic quarters of the mediaeval abbey on [the small island of] Iona and pursued in mission and ministry throughout Scotland and beyond."

"The Community today remains committed to rebuilding the common life, through working for social and political change, striving for the renewal of the church with an ecumenical emphasis, and exploring new more inclusive approaches to worship, all based on an integrated understanding of spirituality".

Chapter 1.
Feed My Sheep

"Alternative Churches: The Future of Religion": Article published by the *Christian Science Monitor* on March 7, 2019. The article can also be viewed on YouTube.

Diana Butler Bass, who teaches at Virginia Theological Seminary (Episcopal), says of Contemplative Worship: This article first appeared in *The Christian Century*, September 19, 2006, pp. 25–29. Copyright by the Christian Century Foundation; used by permission www.christiancentury.org).

Chapter 3.
Order of Service Comparisons

Calvin College designed Lenten Taize Service. Calvin Institute of Christian Worship for the study and renewal of worship. 1855 Knollcrest Circle SE Grand Rapids, MI 49546-4402 USA. (616) 526-6088. Website: worship@calvin.edu. On the campus of Calvin College and Calvin Theological Seminary.

Album *Jesus Remember Me* by the London Fox Taize Choir for the following songs. (See also album *Songs of Taize* by the Taize Community choir. To order songbooks, see the Taize website at www.Taize.fr).

I John 2:7–11 (NIV) Mini homily (one paragraph). Excerpt from sermon, "the One who Loves Lives in the Light," by Rev. John Piper, founder at desiringgod.org:

Prayers of Intercession, Ordinary 20, year A by Alison Holden at www.thisischurch.com. Official Twitter of The World Is Our Parish. Representing St.Marks & Putnoe Heights Churches (Bedford UK) by Rev Canon Royden & Friends.

Chapter 4.
The Iona Abbey Worship Book

The Iona Abbey Worship Book, copyright © 2017, WGRG, The Iona Community and can be obtained by permission from www.ionabooks.org at Wild Goose Publications.

Modern Affirmation of Faith of the Williams Memorial CME (Christian Methodist Episcopal) Temple Church in Shreveport, Louisiana http://wmsmemorialcme.net/:

Chapter 5.
Synthesis of Worship Patterns

The full liturgy of Quiet Service 3A, and Quiet Service 3B and the appendix to services of Quiet 3C, which introduces participants to silent worship, can be found on pages 53-59 of the *Iona Abbey Worship Book*: Copyright © 2017, 2018 WGRG, The Iona Community, 21 Carlton Court, Glasgow, G5 9JP, Scotland.

Chapter 6.

Prayers of Intercession, Ordinary 20, year A by Alison Holden at www.thisischurch.com. Official Twitter of The World Is Our Parish. Representing St.Marks & Putnoe Heights Churches (Bedford UK) by Rev Canon Royden & Friends.

Conclusion.

I John 2:7–11 (NIV) Mini homily (one paragraph). Excerpt from sermon, "the One who Loves Lives in the Light," by Rev. John Piper, founder at desiringgod.org:

[Insert Opening prayer from Iona Quiet Service 3A].

[Insert: Iona blessing from Quiet Service 3A]:

Poem "Pied Beauty" by Gerald Manley Hopkins.

Afterword

YouTube video, "Being the Church in This Time of Pandemic," May 19, 2020. Church leaders discuss the future of the church online: Dr. Diana Butler Bass, The Reverend Joshua Case, The Very Rev Kelvin Holdsworth, and Dr. Deanna A. Thompson.

June 4th, 2020 blog by Gene Veith, titled, *The Newest Church Growth Paradigm: Digital Church*. Vieth quotes from the blog site of church growth expert, Rev. Carey Nieuwhof at Carey Nieuwhof.com.

ADDITIONAL RESOURCES

All Scripture readings are from the NIV Bible and are taken from biblestudytools.com, biblegateway.com and biblehub.com.

Prayers from the BCP refers to the Book of Common Prayer. The Episcopal Church. (New York: Church Hymnal Corp., 1979)

Worship in Song: a Friends Hymnal, © 1966, Friends General Conference, 1216 Arch Street, 2 B, Philadelphia, Pennsylvania 19107.

Chants de Taize, 2018–2019. Copyright © Ateliers et Presses de Taizé, 71250 Taizé, France. All scores available in PDF format at www.taize.fr.

Father Thomas Keating's many books on Contemplation are at Amazon.com. He is the founder of the modern Centering and Contemplative Prayer movement. The book my Contemplation group uses is *The Daily Reader for Contemplative Living, excerpts from the works of Father Thomas Keating*, compiled by S. Stephanie Iachetta. (The Continuum International Publishing Group Inc., New York, NY).

Labyrinth icon front cover. Adaption of labyrinth at Chartres Cathedral found on free images at Clip art.

CPSIA information can be obtained
at www.ICGtesting.com
Printed in the USA
LVHW080011281221
707314LV00019B/482